What You Must Know If You Have Been Arrested For DUI

A Former State Prosecutor's Guide To DUI Charges In Florida

Melinda Morris, Esq., Former State Prosecutor

Seth Shapiro, Esq.

ISBN: 978-1-941645-37-6

DISCLAIMER

This publication is intended to be informational only. No legal advice is being given, and no attorney-client relationship is intended to be created by reading this material. If you are facing legal issues, whether criminal or civil, seek professional legal counsel to get your questions answered.

Note that there may be omissions, out of date information, or errors contained in the book. This book is not a substitute for the live and current legal advice from an attorney based on your specific facts and circumstances.

Morris Law Firm, P.A.

111 2nd Avenue Northeast #515

St. Petersburg, FL 33701

(727) 388-4736

www.criminalattorneystpetersburg.com

CLIENT TESTIMONIALS

"I would recommend Ms. Morris to anyone in the unfortunate position of needing a lawyer. She is completely honest and up front with her clients. She has a deep and personal knowledge of the justice system in Pinellas County. Ms. Morris is also aggressive and tenacious when pursuing one's case. She represented me, and my outcome was exactly as we expected. She will not do wrong by you." **-A DUI Client**

....

"I could not have picked a better attorney. It was nice having someone that actually cared about my case. It was comforting knowing I had a Lawyer representing me where I was a name and not a number. Ms. Morris is very knowledgeable, experienced and personable. Always professional and handled my legal matters quickly and efficiently. She was widely available, promptly returned my phone calls, and always kept me well informed. Her past experience definitely shows. Because of her dedication and hard work on my case the outcome was much better than I expected. I am very satisfied with this firm's services. I highly recommend this firm. I truly appreciate it all. Thanks for everything!!" **- A DUI Client**

....

"Great defense lawyer! Helped me to win my DUI case!"

- A DUI Client

TABLE OF CONTENTS

FOREWORD

From the Editor:

The following book was created with the intent to provide critical information about DUI arrests in Florida to our clients and potential clients. While this information is not a substitute for the direct guidance and counsel of an attorney on your specific facts and circumstances, it may serve to reinforce information you have received from your attorney, or answer questions you may have as you make a decision on retaining an attorney for your DUI case.

This book was created from a series of in-depth interviews with criminal defense attorney and former State Prosecutor Melinda Morris, Esq. of the Morris Law Firm.

The contents herein are presented in an informal and conversational tone as if the reader were listening in on the interview.

We are sorry that you may be reading this book because you or a loved one are going through the unfortunate incident of being charged with a DUI, and hope we can help resolve your case.

Seth Shapiro, Esq.
Morris Law Firm

AUTHOR / ATTORNEY INTRODUCTION

Melinda Morris has been practicing law since 1999 and is the managing attorney of the Morris Law Firm, P.A. As a former Assistant State Attorney with the Sixth Judicial Circuit

in Clearwater, Pinellas County, FL, Ms. Morris has handled thousands of cases from investigation through sentencing. This experience prosecuting cases, along with Ms. Morris' extensive experience as a criminal defense attorney, allows her to aggressively defend her clients.

While a felony prosecutor for the State Attorney's Office in Pinellas County, Ms. Morris prosecuted thousands of criminal cases including DUI, domestic violence, juvenile crimes, and various other misdemeanor and felony offenses. This understanding of the techniques used often by the prosecution has proved invaluable for her criminal defense clients.

Ms. Morris served as a member of the DUI Manslaughter/Vehicular Homicide Squad, a Lead Trial

Attorney, a Domestic Violence Prosecutor, and a Child Abuse Prosecutor. She has participated in over 50 jury trials, and has first-hand experience and jury trials for first-degree murder, manslaughter, capital sexual battery, robbery, DUI Manslaughter, DUI, domestic violence and others.

Ms. Morris attended Stetson University where she received both a Juris Doctorate and a Masters of Business Administration. Stetson University College of Law is ranked No. 1 for trial advocacy and No. 2 for legal writing by U.S. News & World Report and has provided Ms. Morris her outstanding legal foundation.

Ms. Morris' MBA degree in addition to her JD degree enables her to understand the nuances and intricacies of business and corporate procedure, and allows her to provide outstanding representation for those clients accused of White Collar Crimes.

In 2008, Melinda Morris was named a "Rising Star" by the Tampa Bay Times. Ms. Morris is a member of the National Association of Criminal Defense Lawyers, Florida Association of Criminal Defense Lawyers, St. Petersburg Bar Association, Hillsborough County Bar Association, Pinellas Association of Criminal Defense Lawyers, Pinellas County Trial Lawyers Association, Hillsborough County Association of Criminal Defense Lawyers, and the DUI Defense Lawyer's Association.

Do You Think Former Prosecutors Make Better Criminal Defense Attorneys?

It has helped me tremendously to have once worked in the prosecutor's office because you become quite well-trained and experienced with regard to exactly how the State Attorney's Office makes the decision to file criminal charges against defendants, and how to prosecute them, including the strategies, evidence collection and the baseline needed to file charges. You gain a very good understanding of the inner dynamics of how a prosecutor's office works and what they rely on to make decisions.

Knowing these things and being a criminal defense attorney now, trying to defend people who are charged with a crime, it is very helpful with the defense side of the practice. I understand the State Attorney's Office playbook and I understand how the Prosecutors make decisions because I have been on that side of the table.

As a veteran of the State Attorney's Office, you do not benefit with regard to special handouts, but you typically get an audience with the prosecutors within the office because they know you, they take your calls, they know your reputation and the good work that you've done while you were there. All of that can elevate your cases with them and ensure that your voice is heard on behalf of your clients.

WHY DO YOU PRACTICE DUI DEFENSE?

I have been handling DUI cases since 1999, which is when I began as a prosecutor in the State Attorney's Office, and my first trial was a DUI, so I've been handling them for a very long time. When I started my own criminal defense practice, it's something I really wanted to focus on because I find that area of the law very interesting, with many intricate evidentiary issues that aren't present in other areas of the law. Even though DUI is one crime, every person's circumstances are different and the law is constantly evolving and changing, which means every case is different and that keeps it challenging.

DUI cases are the most relatable set of circumstances someone can find themselves in for criminal defense across the board. I've had clients from different professions, backgrounds and ages; DUI affects everyone, and everyone has heard about or known someone who's been involved in it. Sometimes, people find themselves in bad circumstances or having made a bad choice, and other times, they are wrongfully accused based on the misperceptions of an officer.

How Was Your Experience Working With The DUI Manslaughter / Vehicular Homicide Squad?

When I was working for the State Attorney's Office, one thing I was selected to do after I had been there for some time was to serve on what they call the DUI/Manslaughter and Vehicular Homicide Squad, which is something the Pinellas County State Attorney's Office does that is unique to that office. To be selected for the Squad, you must have a certain level of experience on DUI matters. Once on the Squad, if any DUI/manslaughter accidents occur while you are on duty, you are paged and you respond to the scene, which means you help on each case from the very beginning: you start at the scene of the alleged crime with the law enforcement officers, helping decide how to build the case and the evidence that should be collected.

Handling a case this way is unique because you start out at the very beginning, on the ground level at the scene of the crime with the responding officers. As the case progresses, you make the critical decisions all the way up the line, from determining whether or not to formally charge a crime, selecting the appropriate charges to file, being present in court at each stage of the proceedings, and conducting the trial and sentencing where necessary. All of that provides absolutely unique hands-on experience that now, as a defense attorney, can be capitalized on because I have an idea how the prosecutor charges these cases and how law enforcement builds DUI cases.

How Many DUI Cases Have You Handled?

In the thousands because I have been working on DUI cases since 1999. As a prosecutor, I've handled misdemeanor DUIs, felony DUIs and DUI manslaughter cases. As a criminal defense attorney, I've handled misdemeanor DUIs, DUIs with property damage, DUIs with leaving the scene of an accident attached, felony DUIs, serious bodily injury DUIs and DUI manslaughter cases. I've literally handled every kind of DUI case from both sides of the table – as a prosecutor and a criminal defense attorney.

Is There A Stereotypical Client?

Not at all. I've had clients who weren't even 21 years old yet and I have also had clients in their 70s and retired. I've had clients who were a college professor, police officer, lawyer, doctor, teacher, nurse, businessperson – lots of different backgrounds.

How Do People Generally React When They Are Arrested for DUI?

Most people are very scared, and they are stressed out and anxious about what to expect. They have never been involved in the criminal justice system before, they are overwhelmed, and hopefully the benefit of talking with me is that I can explain everything and really break it down and put them at ease as to what I can do and how I can help them through the process.

How Is A DUI Defined In The State Of Florida?

A DUI is defined as when someone is found guilty of driving or being in actual physical control of a vehicle and is under the influence of alcoholic beverages or chemical substance to the extent either their normal faculties are impaired or they have a breath or blood alcohol level that's a .08 or higher - the threshold in Florida. In Florida there are two ways impairment in a DUI case can be proven; either by showing that someone's normal faculties are impaired or that they have a breath or blood alcohol level of .08 or higher. In addition to impairment in a DUI case the State must also prove that the individual was either driving or in actual physical control of the vehicle.

Police can charge someone with DUI based on their normal faculties being impaired alone. For example, I've had clients who have been under the .08 threshold, but have still been arrested and prosecuted for DUI because law enforcement has attempted to show that they were operating the vehicle while their normal faculties were impaired. Law enforcement can still make an arrest even without a breath test based on this same concept of a person's normal faculties being impaired. For example, if you refuse to take a sobriety test when requested by law enforcement there is no breath test, thus law enforcement will pursue the case based on the theory that the person's normal faculties were impaired.

A DUI has both potential criminal and administrative penalties. A DUI case is bifurcated (or split) into these two distinct and separate aspects: the criminal case and the administrative case. The criminal penalties are derived commonly from the misdemeanor (and in some cases felony) charges against the individual that are heard in the criminal court system. The administrative side of the case consists of the penalties that revolve around your driver license and are handled by the Department of Highway Safety Motor Vehicles (DHSMV). It is important to note that one side of the DUI case does not affect the other side – they are completely separate and distinct from one another. For example, receiving an administrative penalty (or suspension) of one's license does not necessarily mean that the person will be found guilty of the DUI case in criminal court. Similarly, avoiding an administrative penalty does not mean that the criminal case will go away. Each side of a DUI case must be defended and resolved separately.

Do Most DUI Clients Have High Breath-Alcohol Levels?

First of all, a fair number of clients have no breath or blood test at all, so they're subject to a normal faculties prosecution because they refused to take the breath test. Approximately half of my DUI clients don't' have a breath test available to quantify a level of impairment because they refused to submit to a breath test.. Of those who have taken the breath test, perhaps half are close to the .08 threshold, and others are inching up toward what would be considered an elevated level. In most DUI cases, you are not seeing someone who is falling down drunk or stumbling around.

What is the Highest Breath or Blood-Alcohol Level Case You Have Handled?

I have handled numerous cases with high breath test results above a .20, and I have had several cases with results above a .30 level. I definitely have represented a significant number of clients with high breath alcohol levels. Occasionally those individuals with high breath tests actually don't look that bad on law enforcement's DUI video because they are regular drinkers, have built up a tolerance and are able to function well even with a high breath alcohol level.

What Are The Common Misconceptions About Being Arrested For A DUI?

Many people assume that because they provided a breath test that was below a .08, or alternatively because they refused to take a breath or blood test, and they feel like they performed well on the field sobriety tests that their DUI charge will just go away. They will assert that they were not drunk, they were not unsteady, stumbling around or falling down, and they are emphatic about their ability to function, so they believe they should be able to get their DUI charge dropped. Unfortunately for them, that is just not how the legal system works at all.

Once a person is charged with DUI, the State Attorney's office will usually aggressively pursue them. The State will rely on the officers who were on the scene, who are trained in DUI enforcement, to testify to their observations that they believe the person's normal faculties were impaired. It's worth noting that law enforcement is judging impairment at a much lower threshold than the public thinks they do. When police officers judge whether or not normal faculties are impaired, they'll give the individual standard field sobriety tests to perform that are not things that anyone does in their normal, everyday life.

No one does that in everyday life, nor do they walk a line, staying on a straight line, heel to toe and make a turn, all the time counting the steps back and forth. Again, those are not common things that people normally do, and people have balance issues, health issues, coordination issues, all of which can affect that test and have nothing to do with impairment, even though the officer will see it that way when he's making the arrest, and he won't generally back down.

The State aggressively pursues DUI cases and prosecutors will strongly support the police officers perception that an individual was driving while impaired and subsequent arrest of them for DUI. Clients come to me with lots of reasonable factors such as they don't have good balance, they're overweight, or they have a health issue, and they'll assert that elements of the field sobriety tests aren't something they can do, and that their poor performance was not an indication of impairment but rather a result of their everyday inability to do these types of movements. Unfortunately, the State will not necessarily take these reasonable factors into account of a person's everyday abilities. An attorney like me is absolutely essential to getting a client's point of view across to the State and presenting their defense to the DUI charge in order to attempt to get the DUI charge to go away since it typically will not get dismissed on its own.

Once you are in the system and you have been charged, it is something that must be litigated and anyone arrested for a DUI really needs a good attorney to advocate for them to get the State Attorney's office to see that they were not impaired and that there were other factors involved.

What Is The Process For An Officer Finding Probable Cause For A DUI Arrest And The State Making A Formal Decision To File Charges?

While the processes can differ in different jurisdictions, there are some commonalities in most DUI arrests and charging decisions.

When an officer stops someone for suspicion of DUI they will conduct an investigation. If the law enforcement officer believes there is probable cause, they will arrest the person for DUI. The probable cause requirement essentially means that law enforcement has a reason to make the arrest. The requirement of probable cause for an arrest comes from the Fourth Amendment of the U.S. Constitution. It should be noted that probable cause required for an arrest is a lower standard than many may think. It simply means that the law enforcement officer must have a reason based on the facts and circumstances that would lead a reasonable person to believe that a crime has been committed. Officers can base probable cause on their general observations of the individual including their performance on field sobriety tests. Oftentimes, a law enforcement officer will note standardized indicators of impairment including observation of bloodshot and watery eyes, slow or slurred speech, odor of alcohol on the person, and other very generalized observations in addition to the individual's performance on the field sobriety tests to establish probable cause. Importantly, it does not take much for law enforcement to establish probable cause for a DUI arrest.

Once the officer has established probable cause they will make the arrest and issue the individual a Florida DUI Uniform Traffic Citation, which charges them under the DUI statute and issues a notice of a court date, which is located on the bottom of the ticket. The individual is then booked, finger printed, and photographed. The officer then files the citation with the Clerk of the Court who puts it into the Court's filing system, and that's how the case gets started.

A misdemeanor DUI is unique in terms of the State Attorney making a filing decision on whether or not to charge the individual with a formal crime. Whereas with other types of offenses, the State Attorney reviews the arresting officer's report before filing a formal charge, with a misdemeanor DUI the individual is formally charged based on the DUI citation. The State Attorney simply relies on the officer's arrest affidavit. There is no formal review by the State Attorney at this stage. Thus, once arrested for a misdemeanor DUI the individual is also formally charged with that crime.

Most misdemeanor DUI cases work this way which is the most common type of DUI case. This includes first-time offenders without any prior DUI charges, and when there is no serious bodily injury or death, which would make it a felony.

So you may be asking yourself, "If I am already formally charged with DUI once I've been arrested, why even hire an attorney?" It is a good question, and the answer is of critical importance. First, even though you may be officially charged with DUI, an attorney may still be able to get your charges dropped or reduced based on a thorough review of the evidence against you and aggressive negotiation with the State Attorney's Office.

The process of formal charging only works this way for a DUI. If for example someone is charged with petty theft, possession of marijuana or battery and then there would be a window of time between when they are arrested and when they are formally charged with a crime by the State Attorney. In these instances the case gets referred to the State Attorney's Office where a prosecutor is assigned, and then there will be an investigatory period during which we, as attorneys, can get involved, advocate for our client to try to present evidence as to why we don't think they committed a crime, and try to convince the prosecutor not to file charges (also referred to as filing a No Information).

Misdemeanor DUI charges absolutely do not work like that but instead occupy their own unique area of the law in that they do not go to a prosecutor; rather they are triggered by that citation from the police officer and there is no investigatory period with the State Attorney's office during which they decide whether or not to charge you. Now, if you are arrested for a felony DUI that works different in that the State is required to conduct an investigation before proceeding on a felony case. If arrested for a felony DUI then you should definitely contact the Morris Law Firm to help you because we do have a window of time while the State is investigating to present mitigating evidence to them in order to get the DUI case dropped down to a misdemeanor charge.

What Are Standard Field Sobriety Tests? Can Someone Refuse Them?

Before a police officer can ask someone to perform Field Sobriety Tests (FSTs) they must have an objective basis to make a traffic stop, and then a reasonable suspicion that a DUI has been committed or is being committed to start a criminal investigation for DUI. Typically, an officer pulls someone over for suspected impairment, whether they are speeding, driving too slowly, driving the wrong way or with no headlights on - although the most common scenario is because they are seen weaving in and out of their lane. That gives the officer what is called an objective basis for the stop - they have observed some sort of traffic infraction and they pull the driver over for that traffic infraction. That is exactly what the officer will report to the prosecutor on the case - that they stopped the driver for a specific traffic infraction as the basis for the stop.

Once an individual has been pulled over, they will be asked questions, with the most common being where they came from and whether or not they had anything to drink. Typically, if someone answers that they have had an alcoholic drink, the police officer will indicate they smelled alcohol, or that the person's eyes were bloodshot and glassy, and then state they suspected impairment as a basis to initiate a DUI investigation. Next, the police officer will have the individual step out of the car and perform a Horizontal Gaze Nystagmus Test, or HGN on them. HGN is a standardized field sobriety test in which the officer will use a pen and measure the individual's eyes, to detect impairment by looking for the onset of what's called nystagmus (an involuntary movement of the eyes), because law enforcement believes the onset of nystagmus relates to impairment.

Research that law enforcement relies on indicates that if someone has been drinking alcohol and they are at a blood-alcohol level above .08, they will have a certain level of nystagmus, which is an eye spasm and will show when the officer is measuring the eyes with the pen test. I don't see it happen often, but if law enforcement did a HGN test and there was no sign of impairment they would probably just let the individual go back in their car, write a citation for the traffic infraction and send them on their way. Of course, if the officer believes the HGN test shows signs of impairment, they will perform additional standardized field sobriety tests.

Everyone has the right to refuse FSTs; there is no mandatory requirement that a person has to perform field sobriety tests. Note that refusal to submit to FSTs is differentiated from refusal to submit to a breath test (discussed below). The officer is required to warn the person that their refusal to perform FSTs will be used against them when the case is prosecuted in court. Most of the time people feel like they need to cooperate, so they comply and take the FSTs which usually consists of the Walk And Turn Test, and the One Leg Stand Test. Other FSTs may be incorporated including the Finger to Nose Test, but these are less common.

The officer will usually start with the Walk And Turn test. The officer will use a line that's available on the road, or if there isn't one, he will use chalk or tape to draw one. The Walk and Turn test consists of the officer providing instructions on how to perform the test while the individual has been instructed to stand in the "starting position." The starting position is an unnatural stance with feet positioned heel to toe with one's arms down by the sides. Not only is this position unnatural, it is also inherently unstable. Unfortunately, the ability to stay perfectly still and balanced is measured by the officer while he goes through what is typically a long-winded and potentially confusing set of directions. In nearly all instances, the individual will be instructed to take nine (9) heel to toe steps on the line while counting out each step, and then perform an unnatural and unnecessarily complex turning pattern that consists of keeping one foot planted while using the other foot to pivot around the planted foot. Then the individual is instructed to return down the line heel to toe for another nine steps while again counting out loud each step taken. Any failure to step exactly heel to toe, count out loud, or perform the turn exactly as instructed is counted against the individual. Additionally, using arms for balance or any failure to stay on the line, swaying, tripping, or falling will be counted as an indicator of impairment even if it is due to a physical deficiency unrelated to impairment.

The next test is typically the One Leg Stand Test. The One Leg Stand test consists of the officer providing instructions to the individual while they are again placed in a starting position with feet together and arms by the sides. The individual is then instructed to raise one foot (of their choice) off of the ground approximately six (6) inches with the foot parallel to the ground, arms by the sides. Then the individual is instructed to count while the foot is raised until the officer instructs them to stop. The officer will be looking for any swaying, use of arms for balance, putting the raised foot down, hopping to keep balance, or falling over. Additionally, individuals naturally start the exercise before the officer formally instructs them to begin, which is also counted as a failure to follow instructions.

Most of the time, if you are in good health and of normal, average weight and there is nothing unusual about you or your circumstances, the Walk And Turn and the One Leg Stand Test are the two FSTs officers will utilize. Based on the results of these two tests and their overall observations of the interaction, the officer will determine if they've found enough clues of impairment, and if so they will make an arrest for DUI.

If someone is older, over the age of 65, if they appear to be more than 50 pounds overweight, or if they explain that have some sort of physical limitation or medical condition, officers can give alternative FSTs, such as the

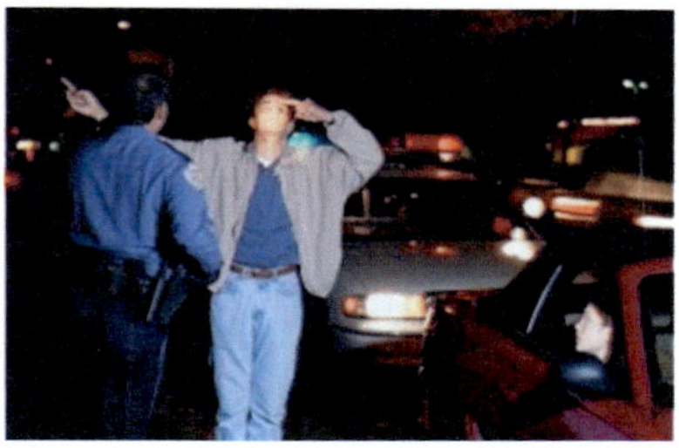

Finger To Nose Test, in which you are instructed to touch the tip of your nose with the tip of your finger, or the Romberg Alphabet Test, in which they ask the person to recite the alphabet, to see if that can be done without missing any letters. Officers can administer these alternative FSTs in certain circumstances, and based on their observations can also make an arrest for DUI.

What Are The Common Issues People Face With Field Sobriety Tests?

There are numerous issues people have with Field Sobriety Tests (FSTs). From the physical difficulty of performing the actual tests, to understanding and being able to follow the officer's very specific instructions during a time of great stress and anxiety, the tests are setup to fail.

On the Walk And Turn test police give you instructions, place you in the starting position with one foot directly in front of the other, all the while having your arms by your side. They continue to instruct you to walk nine steps down the line counting the whole time, then perform a turn, and finally walk nine more steps back exactly the same way, counting the steps out loud, without using your arms for balance.

Officers will be looking at many different things - if you step off the line, if you don't touch heel to toe, if you use your arms for balance, if you count the incorrect number of steps, if you do an improper turn - and they will count those as errors. If you miss two or more items, they will deem that you have failed the test, and use that as a basis to arrest you for DUI.

For the One Leg Stand Test, officers allow you to choose which leg to stand on and tell you to pick the other leg up off the ground with your arms at your side while you look down at your feet and counting the seconds, with the goal being 30 seconds. You have to look at your foot while keeping it off the ground with your arms at your side and not using them for balance, and if you can't do all of that, or if you fall over or stumble or lose your balance, they will consider any of those to be clues of impairment and if you get two or more errors, you will have failed the test and they'll arrest you for DUI.

One of the biggest issues with both tests is the instructions which must be followed to the letter. Additionally, the physical movements required during the tests are very unnatural. Much of what an individual is asked to do is very challenging, to the point that someone may think they performed the tests well, but

the officer's observation will say otherwise. For example, standing on one leg is not something people are used to doing, and it's very unnatural to look down at your foot while you're attempting to hold that position. Most people will gaze off into the distance and try to find a point to reference for balance, which you're not allowed to do during the test. Again, someone may believe they did fine, but the officer says they missed a number of elements and those can end up being issues for some clients.

The key is that it all comes down to that officer's perception. Quite frankly, much of the time when you're stopped for weaving in and out of your lane and you say you had been out with some friends, and that you had a couple of beers, the officer will be predisposed to view your performance on those tests a certain way, meaning he's looking for evidence of DUI and he plans to arrest you for that because that's his perception.

Often, you're by yourself and you've never been arrested before and, naturally a person is much more intimidated and nervous than if they had only been pulled over for a speeding ticket. Most people are upset about getting a ticket, but just imagine how much worse it is to be stopped late at night when you're by yourself and you've never been arrested before, and all of a sudden the officer's asking you to do all of these tests.

Field Sobriety Tests are a very important. They are possibly one of the most important tests of your life because based on how you perform the officer will decide whether he has enough to arrest you. If you think about every other test you have taken in your life you get a lot of preparation time. Even for your basic driving test, you have plenty of time to prepare for it. In school you get to prepare for your tests and have time to study.

Yet here, with Field Sobriety Tests you are put on the spot with no preparation time whatsoever in an incredibly stressful situation where the potential outcome isn't just a poor grade – it is going to jail. It's not normal to be stopped by an officer, be put on the spot, with just a minute or two of quick instruction. You are supposed to remember everything that the officer tells you to do and do it in the correct order, the exact way he tells you to do it, and if you don't do it exactly right, you're arrested. That's a confusing, stressful and intimidating situation for many people to find themselves in.

What Is The Breath Test? How Reliable Is It?

You will not be required to do a breath test until after you've been arrested. That is the law. If the officer requires a breath test before a formal arrest it could be a basis to exclude the breath test from evidence. Typically, an officer makes a stop, asks some questions, pulls you out of the car, requests you to perform some field sobriety tests and judges your performance and then decides whether he has probable cause and, if he thinks he does, he arrests you. Only after that arrest for DUI are you asked if you will submit to a breath test.

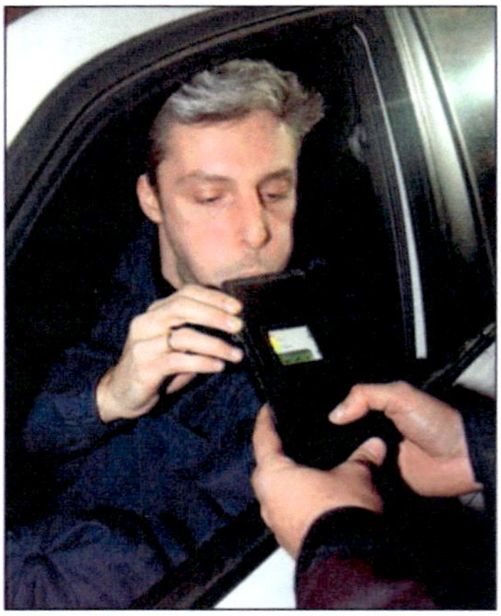

What many people don't realize is that the breath test comes into the equation only after the arrest. Furthermore, even if you take the breath test and the result is under the legal limit of .08, the officer can't and won't un-arrest you. You must still go to court and answer for the arrest and what happens with your DUI case will be up to the prosecutor. Taking that breath test does not change your fate at that point. You are already under arrest for DUI and that will not be undone.

The breath test itself can happen on the roadside or back at the station.

For most cases handled in the Tampa Bay area, once you are arrested you are taken back to either the police department, or the sheriff's office can take you to the jail where you will be requested to take the breath test. There are also some officers with a portable breath test machine in their trunk, so they can request you submit to a breath test right there on scene.

When the breath test is offered back at the station or at the jail there is a time delay of up to an hour or more between being stopped and when you're given the breath test. It is important to note this delay because alcohol metabolizes in an individual's system resulting in a breath test measurement that is potentially greater than a measurement taken closer to the time of the incident.

Finally, many people think that a DUI stop begins with an officer administering a portable breath test. That is not what happens. A DUI investigation and arrest takes place first with the breath test following after the arrest.

What Are The Potential Consequences Of Refusing A Breath Test?

In Florida, if you refuse to take the breath test, there will be an administrative suspension of your driver license for 12 months for a first refusal and 18 months for a second refusal. Typically, if you agree to take a breath test and the result is above a .08 (the legal limit in Florida) there is a 6-month administrative suspension of your license. It is an administrative suspension because the suspension is through and by the Department of Highway Safety Motor Vehicles (DHSMV), which is the administrative agency that issued your driver license.

In Florida, consenting to a breath test is actually part of an agreement with the DHSMV in exchanging for them granting you the privilege to drive. In fact, on the bottom of the driver license there's a statement in small print that says, "Operation of a motor vehicle constitutes consent to any sobriety test required by law." This is known as the implied consent law. Any person who accepts the privilege of operating a motor vehicle, by operating such vehicle, is deemed to have given his or her consent to submit to an approved test incident to a lawful arrest for DUI.

Think of this like a contractual agreement between you, as the driver, and the DHSMV. In return for being able to drive on Florida roads, if an officer stops you and has a reasonable basis to suspect that you are impaired, and then asks you to take a breath test you are giving your implied consent to take that test. If you refuse under these circumstances to take a breath test, the DHSMV will issue a 12-month administrative suspension of your driver license.

In short, you will receive a six-month administrative driver license suspension if you take the breath test and you are above the legal limit, but a 12 month administrative suspension will be imposed if you simply refuse to take the breath test.

When Are Blood Tests Typically Administered Instead Of The Breath Test?

A blood test is used if a breath test isn't practical or is impossible. For example, if there is an accident and the person is transported to the hospital the officer can't administer a breath test in such a scenario, thus they can

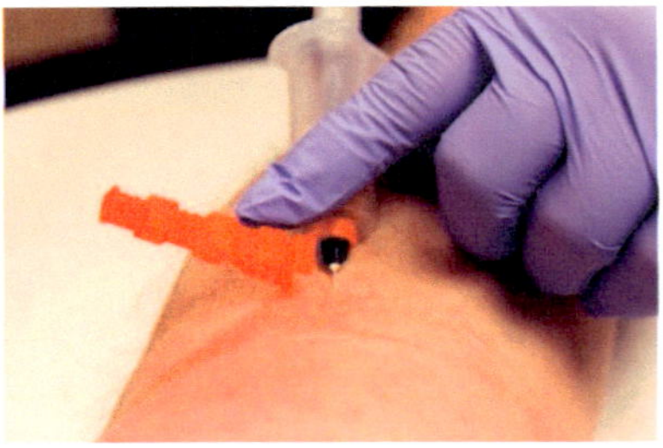

ask that person to agree to submit to a blood test. Again, as long as it is a misdemeanor DUI case you can refuse to submit to a blood test, just like a breath test.

However, if you're in an accident and you cause serious bodily injury or death to another person, and the police suspect you were driving impaired then law enforcement can take your blood without permission. In those instances, the police can do a forcible blood draw, although they must have a basis to believe there is impairment; they can't just take a blood test for no reason.

What Are Some Common Defense Strategies Against Field Sobriety, Breath and Blood Tests?

Field sobriety tests are always recorded on video and defense counsel will always order the video and watch it. I am looking to see how a client did on those tests. I am not looking for exactly how the officer instructed them to do it, and I am not looking to see if a client walks exactly nine or even ten steps, or if do they do the turn exactly right. I just want to see if generally their balance looks good and they're not swaying, stumbling or falling. In summary, I am not looking for perfection on these tests but rather I am determining if their overall demeanor and appearance is not one of impairment.

I want to see if they're able to maintain walking the line and perhaps they'll count ten steps instead of nine but that can be a common habit and not necessarily impairment. When I look at the video, I will try to determine if there's an overall sense of whether they are impaired, or if they just didn't get every direction that was given to them within that one to two minute instruction period.

If I think the client looks pretty good, and they didn't really understand each instruction because it was given to them quickly, or it wasn't explained very well, or they tell me they have health issues (for example they're overweight and just weren't physically capable of performing the test), that's where I can start picking it apart and make the argument to a judge or a jury that they don't come across as impaired and that the problem is in the way the officer conducted the tests. Perhaps the officer gave the instructions too quickly, maybe not enough time was spent ensuring the person understood, or maybe they're in a very distracting environment.

Sometimes people are in the middle of a parking lot where other people are going in and out of a business and watching them, or you can hear cars driving by, or the weather conditions are unfavorable. All of these are factors that can be presented on that person's behalf to say that these aren't normal conditions in which to perform these types of tests, and so they're not really measuring your normal faculties, and within that environment, they did as well as anyone could expect. The argument becomes that they're not impaired at the time; they're just performing how anyone would do with the limitations or issues when the test was administered.

What Are Some Things That Can Go Wrong With The Breath Test?

In Florida, the Intoxilyzer 8000 manufactured by CMI is the most commonly used breath test machine. The Intoxilyzer needs to be properly maintained and calibrated to produce accurate and reliable test results. There have been various reports throughout Florida of Intoxilyzer machines not being properly maintained and calibrated, and of improper use of the machines themselves.

The Florida Department of Law Enforcement is supposed to keep all of the records regarding how that maintenance is conducted, so one thing I look at whenever someone actually takes a breath test is the maintenance records to ensure that machine has been properly maintained. There have been documented issues in some counties with different agencies who are in charge of these machines who are not necessarily doing what they're supposed to do to properly maintain the machines.

Sometimes the defense can go after the police officers with the portable breath test machines because they are driving around with these devices in their car, going over bumps, pot holes and being in the heat all day which makes them susceptible to mechanical issues.

The time the breath test is taken can also be a factor. Breath test results can fluctuate based on the amount of time from the last alcoholic beverage consumed to the time of the test. Often, if I have a client with a breath test that is very close to .08, I can perform an extrapolation and make the prosecution prove they were at a .08 or higher while driving, not just when they took the breath test, which can be some time after they were stopped. If I extrapolate this backwards, I can show that perhaps they were below the legal limit at the time of driving and I can attack the DUI charge on those grounds.

When people come to me with a refusal the favorite argument of the prosecutor is what is called a "consciousness of guilt" argument – that someone will only refuse to take the breath test because they know they won't pass it because they had too much to drink and would blow above .08. I always try to refute that and show there are many other reasons for someone not to take a breath test. These reasons can include a lack of trust in accuracy of the machines and previous advice from other people that tell them not to take a breath test under any circumstances. Many people just don't understand what to do - they've never been arrested before, they're overwhelmed and confused and they don't have the opportunity to talk to an attorney before making the decision to take a breath test.

In an abundance of caution, because police have usually read Miranda, and the person understands that they have the right to not make any statements at that time, people often choose not to take the breath test. It might not have anything to do with how much they've had to drink, or a consciousness of guilt, or whether or not they think they can pass it, but just that other life experiences are influencing them to not take the breath test.

How Much Training Do Police Officers Have Regarding Field Sobriety, Breath And Blood Tests?

They typically receive the most basic training as part of their law enforcement training at the police academy. Most of officers take a 40-hour class, and those 40 hours are split up between traffic stops, field sobriety tests, and breath tests. When you think about it, that is not a lot of training given the potential consequences to the individual resting on the competency of the officer. Most officers get their real experience with DUI stops as on the job experience that can also lead to issues with how the stops and tests are administered.

What Is The Process After A DUI Arrest In Florida?

Once you're arrested, you'll be taken back to the police station and asked to take a breath test, after which you'll be taken to the jai. In some cases you'll be taken straight to the jail and asked to go to the central breath testing room for the breath test. Either way, after the breath test, you'll be booked into jail, where you must be held for at least eight hours before you can be released, since that's the length of time deemed long enough for alcohol to clear out of someone's system. You may not think you're drunk at all, or you may be extremely drunk and three times the legal limit - it does not matter - everyone who's arrested and booked for DUI is required by law to spend eight hours in jail before they can be bonded out or released on their own recognizance.

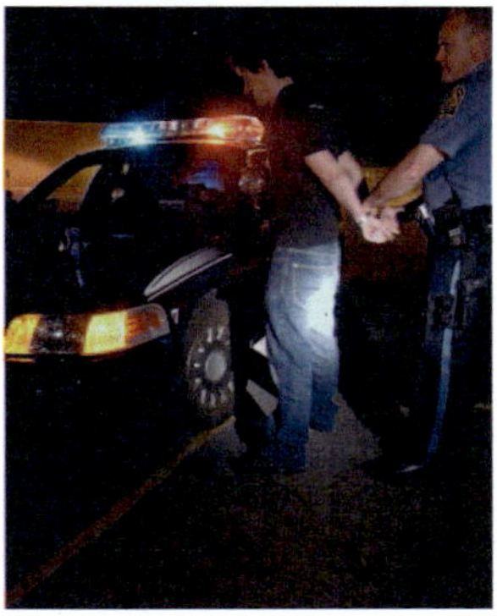

When Can Someone Get A Lawyer Involved In This Process?

Once released from jail, you are given a copy of the DUI citation and at the bottom is a court date, which is an arraignment hearing. From the minute you are released from jail, you should be looking for an attorney, because you should never represent yourself. The average person has no legal experience, and no experience with DUIs. You should consider hiring an attorney and preparing for the first court date.

There are two things to be concerned with when you are charged with a DUI - one is the criminal charge of DUI, which should be defended by an attorney well before the first court date. The other is the potential suspension of your driver license. When arrested for DUI, law enforcement seizes your driver license. When you are released from jail, you are provided a Florida DUI Uniform Traffic Citation with the court date at the bottom. This citation acts as your temporary driver license for 10 days. Within this 10-day timeframe, you must deal with the potential administrative suspension of your driver license. An attorney can provide the appropriate guidance for your specific circumstances to deal with the DHSMV's suspension process. If you do not proactively address the potential administrative suspension of your driver license it will automatically be suspended for six months if you've taken the breath test and the results are over .08, or 12-months – 18 months if you've refused the breath test.

I advise clients that obviously we have to be concerned about the court date, and we want to be prepared to handle the criminal side of the case, but we also have to decide within the first 10 days after the arrest as what to do with the DHSMV in regard to your driver license suspension.

What Is The Driver's License Suspension Process?

In Florida, you face a six-month administrative suspension if you took a breath test and the result was over a .08, or a 12-18 month suspension for a refusal of the breath test. The officer seizes your driver license at the time of the arrest and puts it with the DUI Arrest Packet, which is a collection of all documents the officer is relying on to support the arrest. This arrest packet includes the citation issued, the arrest affidavit, the police report, a copy of your breath test results or a refusal affidavit, a field sobriety observation checklist showing how you performed on the FSTs, and typically a form with which the officer signs under oath stating that everything in the packet is true and correct, and that the officer is relying on that information to support the license suspension.

The officer then turns the DUI Arrest Packet and the seized driver license over to the Department of Motor Vehicles, which triggers the suspension of your license. As mentioned, you only have 10 days from the date of your arrest to deal with the potential driver license suspension.

If you are a first time DUI offender, you have two choices; you can either go to the DMV and fill out a form waiving your right to a hearing to contest the suspension and get a hardship license, which is formally referred to as a business purpose only license (BPO), which allows people to drive to work, to church, to school, or other necessities of daily life, like a doctor's appointment, but not allow driving for social engagements.

Some people will hire an attorney to fight the criminal case, but it's important to be able to keep driving to work so they don' t lose their job on top of the other potential consequences, so they just waive their right to fight the DHSMV suspension. It is important to know that whatever you do through the DHSMV the consequence is administrative and it has no bearing at all on your DUI criminal case. In fact, typically the criminal courts have no knowledge of what's going on administratively through the DHSMV, just as the DHSMV is not concerned and has no knowledge of what's going on with the criminal case.

On the other hand, if you decide you want to have an Administrative Review Hearing in front of a hearing officer at the DHSMV to challenge the administrative license suspension, your attorney will do that for you, since it is part the representation on the DUI. I not only defend clients in criminal court, but I also have a very thorough discussion about the DHSMV consequences to your driver license, and whether you want to challenge the suspension. If a client decides to challenge the administrative suspension, I will file for a formal review hearing. Our firm takes care of the filing fee and files a notice with the DHSMV requesting a formal review hearing. I will also order a copy of your DUI Arrest Packet, to see if there is a basis to challenge your administrative driver license suspension.

When an Administrative Review Hearing is elected, the DHSMV issues a temporary driving permit so that you can drive while awaiting the hearing. At the hearing, the DHSMV can make one of two decisions: they may decide to overturn the suspension, saying the officer had no basis to issue the suspension, perhaps because there was no probable cause for the arrest, or there's not enough evidence that you were actually driving, or perhaps the officer made some procedural mistakes in the arrest packet and the DHSMV deems the packet insufficient evidence to rely on for the suspension. If the DHSMV overturns the suspension, they will put an Order back into the DHSMV database and you can go back to the DMV and get your driver license again, with no restrictions at all.

Of course, the DHSMV may uphold the suspension, and conclude that the officer acted appropriately and did everything correctly. When that happens, the temporary permit that they issued has an expiration date and when that expires you'll have either a 30-day hard suspension if you took the breath test or a 90-day hard suspension if you refused the breath test. This hard suspension is akin to a penalty for choosing to have an Administrative Review Hearing and not winning. A hard suspension means you cannot drive for any reason whatsoever, but then, when that hard suspension period has expired, you can apply for the BPO license.

The decision between electing to have an Administrative Review Hearing versus simply obtaining a BPO license immediately all comes down to talking to the client and determining the risks and what is best for the client's individual circumstances. Some clients can't chance losing the Administrative Review Hearing because if they lose, they will have to go 30 or 90 days on the hard suspension period with no driving which could cause them to lose their job, so they choose to waive their right to the hearing and take the BPO license from day one. In these cases the client accepts the administrative suspension being a part of their driving record permanently in exchange for the ability to drive on the BPO license.

Other clients feel differently - they not only want to fight the criminal case, but the administrative case as well. These clients decide it is worth the risk of going 30 or 90 days without driving on a hard suspension if they lose the Administrative Review Hearing just in order to have an opportunity to have the administrative suspension overturned. Perhaps they have other transportation, or they can ride a bike or walk. To these clients it is important to challenge every aspect of the DUI case – both administrative and criminal. This decision is one that we have to make very early on in the case because we only have 10 days from the date of the arrest.

The ability to forgo the Administrative Review Hearing and elect a BPO license is only available to first time DUI offenders. If you have any prior DUI arrests you have no choice - you must file for the Administrative Review Hearing because the benefit of the immediate BPO license is only available to those with no prior DUI history.

What Happens If You Win The Administrative Review Hearing?

If you win the Administrative Review Hearing the DHSMV puts an Order back in the DMV database and you can get your license reinstated with no restrictions at all, although this only applies to the administrative suspension.

Once you go to court, if several months down the road you are convicted of DUI, you will face a criminal suspension of your driver license that the judge orders as part of the DUI sanctions.

All process and procedure through the DHSMV regarding the Administrative Review Hearing is a very intricate and complicated process. It is very difficult to get through this process and minimize any potential administrative sanctions or loss of driving privileges if you attempt to do this yourself. The benefit of hiring an attorney who's experienced is that we can walk you through the process, explain all of the options, and ensure that you make the right decision for your individual circumstances.

What Are Ignition Interlock Devices And How Are They Used In Florida?

In Florida, if you take a breath test and the result is .08 to just under .15, there are non-enhanced sanctions. However, if your breath test result is a .15 or higher it is considered an enhanced DUI, and you are subject to higher sanctions, including a more significant fine, as well as the requirement of an ignition interlock device on any car you drive for six months. This is true even for a first time DUI offender. For a second DUI, regardless of your blood-alcohol level, or if you refuse the breath test on a second DUI, you are required to have an ignition interlock device. These requirements may change depending on when your previous DUI occurred.

The most common reason that people with a first time DUI will be required to have an ignition interlock device is because they registered a breath or blood-alcohol level of .15 or higher. The benefit of hiring an attorney is that if your breath test result registered between a .15 and a .19, we will do everything we can to persuade the State Attorney's Office to reduce the DUI to under a .15 so there are no enhancements such as the ignition interlock device.

One method of convincing the State to reduce the DUI case to one with a breath test result under .15 is to perform an extrapolation report for the client. Extrapolation reports are useful in cases where the client's breath test result was just above a .15, but there was a significant gap in time between the traffic stop and the breath test measurement. Extrapolation allows us to determine what the breath test result would have been at the time of the stop that may be significantly less than the result of the measurement taken some time after the traffic stop. With this report, evidence can be presented and the argument made that, at the time of driving, you would have been under .15, but because of the delay in the breath test, your alcohol level continued to rise, and it peaked out at the time of the measurement. If successful the requirement of the ignition interlock device can be avoided for the client.

What Are The Challenges Regarding Prescription Drug DUI Cases?

While DUI cases involving alcohol are definitely more prevalent I see a fair number of prescription drug cases as well. They are very difficult cases because a doctor has usually prescribed the client those medications, and they are taking the medications as prescribed. Thus, the client does not feel like they're doing anything wrong. At the same time, however, an officer is adamant that they were impaired and that those medications affected their ability to drive. This typically results in a conflict between the State Attorney's Office making the argument that the client is impaired due to the prescription medications, and our argument that the medications were legally prescribed by a physician, the client needed these medications according to their doctor and took as directed according to the doctor, and they had no reason to believe they were impaired or intent to drive while impaired.

WHAT CAN ENHANCE OR AGGRAVATE DUI CHARGES IN FLORIDA?

First and foremost, if your alcohol level is elevated, it will be a major factor, but other factors can lead to an enhanced or aggravated DUI as well, such as if there's a crash involved, if you have a child in the car, or if the video of the stop and the arrest shows clients making derogatory or very negative statements towards the officers. Any prior history of DUI will also aggravate your case and enhance it.

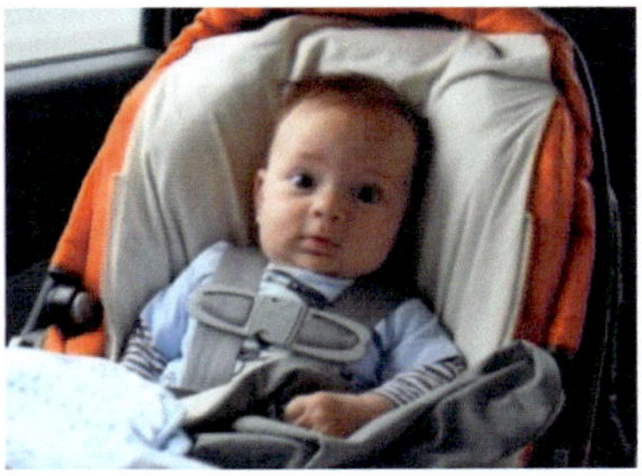

Do Most DUI Cases Go To Trial Or Are They Settled?

Whether a case goes to trial or is settled and pled out depends on the client. Some clients just don't want to go to trial under any circumstances. Others are willing to take the risk in exchange for the potential reward. In cases where I can get the charges amended to a lower level crime, such as reckless driving or careless driving that can be a better outcome for the client and they wish to resolve it with that outcome rather than go to trial with an unknown result.

Outside of plea bargaining, there are other strategies to help minimize the negative consequences that are typically associated with a DUI. I most often have the client complete certain requirements up front, proactively. Thus, by the time we get in front of a judge for sentencing, the client has completed many of the requirements under the DUI statute, which helps lessen the impact of the sentence itself, and may allow the judge to lessen the duration of time under supervision.

The significance of hiring an experienced attorney is the knowledge that the attorney is not afraid to take the case to trial if necessary. Many attorneys don't or won't take cases to trial because they don't have the necessary experience, or they are simply not comfortable with the process, so they will often just plea bargain the case with the State Attorney without pressing the case as far as it needs to go in order to achieve the best result.

It's only those attorneys with significant DUI trial experience, along with the background and the willingness to take a case all the way to trial that can press the case and achieve the best result for the client. The State very well knows which attorneys have that capability and do well in trial and which attorneys will avoid trial at all costs. Trial experience should be a significant factor when a client is making a hiring decision because even if a client never intends to go to trial having an attorney with a reputation for trial helps achieve a better outcome in the client's case.

What Are The Potential Sentences For First Time DUI & Multiple Time DUI Offenders?

If I cannot get a case dropped or reduced to some other offense outside of a DUI, a client may face a DUI sentence. A typical sentence for a first time offender is an adjudication (finding) of guilt, which is mandatory on any DUI sentence in Florida. This means that you are being convicted of the DUI charge and you will be a convicted criminal. The judge has no discretion in the matter; when a person is sentenced to a DUI in Florida the law requires an adjudication of guilt. This is unlike other criminal offenses where a sentencing judge may order a withhold of adjudication meaning that the court is providing a disposition on the case, but is simply withholding judgment as to guilt or innocence which is typically a very good result for most clients.

In terms of consequences along with an adjudication of guilt on a first time DUI, the standard sentence is a 12-month period of criminal probation, and a fine of approximately $1000. If you have an enhanced breath test, above a .15, the fine will increase to approximately $1500.

A first time DUI conviction also carries a 6-month criminal suspension of your driver license. You will also be required to complete DUI school, and complete an alcohol abuse evaluation. If it is determined during the evaluation that you need counseling, you'll also have to complete that counseling. Additionally, 50 hours of community service are required, although some judges will let you buy out that community service, while some will not. The judge may also order you to complete a Victim Impact Panel, which is a three-hour course put on by Mothers Against Drunk Driving (MADD), with speakers who have been victimized by DUI drivers.

There will also be a 10 day impound of your vehicle, during which you can't drive your vehicle for any reason. The judge will also typically order you not to consume any alcohol or go to any bars or clubs while you're on probation. Further, you will have to pay any investigative costs that are claimed by your arresting agency.

For an enhanced DUI with a breath test result above a .15, you will be required to have an ignition interlock device installed on your vehicle for a period of six months.

On a second DUI that occurs within five years of the first DUI, you'll face mandatory jail time, and there will be higher fines, a five-year driver license suspension, and a longer ignition interlock requirement. If your second DUI is outside of five years, you will still face the higher fine, and possibly a longer driver's license suspension and ignition interlock, but there isn't any mandatory jail time.

If you receive a third DUI within 10 years, you'll have more mandatory jail time, a longer driver's license suspension, and a higher fine. Overall everything will be more significant and may be enhanced even more by your blood-alcohol level. A third or a fourth DUI can also be prosecuted as a felony in Florida.

Are Alternative Programs Available For First Time DUI Offenders?

If you are facing mandatory jail time on your DUI case because you are a multiple offender the only legal substitution for jail time that a judge can exercise is a residential alcohol treatment program. Legally , residential treatment is the only alternative to jail that's allowed. If you are in a first time DUI situation there's no mandatory jail but if the prosecutors or the judge wants someone to go to jail because there are aggravators in that case (perhaps an extremely high breath test, or there was a crash, or a child in the car, or maybe you just displayed bad behavior towards the officers, or there's something inflaming the judge) an experienced attorney always attempts to negotiate for alternatives to jail time in these circumstances.

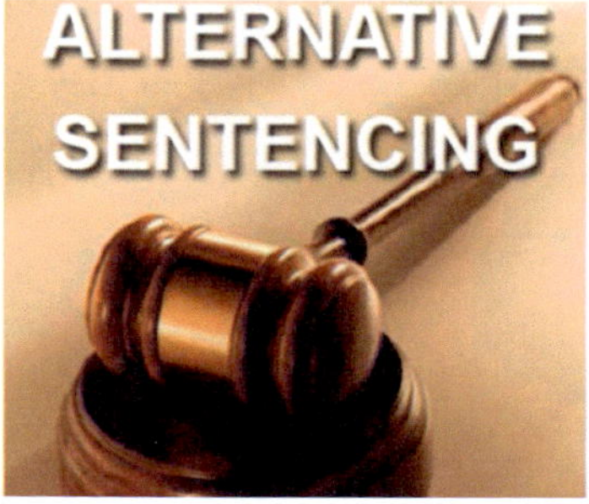

One alternative is a Continuous Alcohol Monitor (CAM) that is placed on your ankle that monitors for alcohol consumption, or a device called a Sober Link, which is basically a very small, handheld breathalyzer device with which you can submit a breath test reading multiple times each day while being monitored.

The above alcohol monitoring devices can assure the judge that you're being monitored for alcohol and complying with sentencing. If the device alerts that you've consumed alcohol, the court can actually have a pickup order issued and you can be taken to jail. Alcohol monitoring is a way to keep a client out of jail, while at the same time giving the judge a feeling that they can monitor the person and their alcohol consumption.

Can Someone Represent Themselves in A DUI Case?

If you represent yourself (called pro se), it is unlikely to turn out well for you because most non-attorneys do not have any experience in criminal law or DUI law. You do not know the prosecutor or the judge and you don't know what they're expecting. Frankly, I don't think the State will give you any benefit because they have the upper hand and the advantage in that situation.

Unfortunately, with the public defender's office, they have great attorneys who work there, but they also have an extremely high caseload. The Public Defender is typically overworked and overburdened and they can't dedicate as much time to each individual client as a private defense attorney can. They also can tend to get cases later in the process, which can sometimes work as a disadvantage to the client.

How Do You Convince Clients Not To Plead Guilty To A DUI ?

I definitely discourage anyone from pleading guilty on their own because when you do that you can potentially get the maximum possible sanctions. On the other hand, when you come to the judge with the benefit of an attorney who will advocate for you, and ensure that you have proactively completed the DUI sentencing requirements such as DUI school, alcohol treatment, and community service the judge may use more discretion in sentencing. If you haven't proactively completed the DUI sanctions the judge has to give you the maximum term of supervision to ensure that you complete those requirements while on criminal probation.

Additionally, if you don't hire an attorney then you don't have the benefit of an experienced counsel digging through your case to see if there are weaknesses in the evidence or the case that can be challenged. Instead, you would just be going in and receiving a DUI conviction which will have an impact on your background and driving record along with possible enhancements if you ever receive another DUI in the future.

Further, a DUI in Florida carries a mandatory adjudication so you'll become a convicted criminal without the benefit of an attorney to help you through it, and you're putting yourself in a position where that criminal conviction could haunt you for the rest of your working life. Your current job may not care, but if you go on to get another job they'll pull your record, and it may in fact be used against you during the hiring process. We've seen parents for whom it's become an issue when they're subject to background screens to volunteer in their children's classroom or go on field trips.

We have also seen people who have issues with housing because apartment complexes do a background check to see if you have a criminal record and when they see a DUI, you could have a problem. A DUI conviction can have a tremendous long-term effect on you, so making the impulsive decision to just throw yourself on the mercy of the court is not beneficial to you in the long run.

It should be emphasized that hiring an attorney who knows the State Attorney's process and can have their clients proactively go to the DUI school, begin counseling and perform some of the other DUI requirements is beneficial. This way, when the client goes court the attorney can show you in a more positive light and present that you are taking the issue seriously.

Taking the appropriate steps proactively is very important because the judge may view this as a mitigating factor. Only attorneys with a background in DUI cases and deep experience to know what to have their clients do can effectively achieve this for their clients.

DOES A CLEAN RECORD AND GOOD CHARACTER HELP A DUI CASE?

A clean record in and of itself unfortunately does not help you very much, although, in combination with other factors that can be argued regarding your case it may assist in resolving your case. For example, if you are a great person with a good job, perhaps you volunteer significantly in the community, and you have a great deal of support from family and friends those facts can be incorporated into your defense as mitigating factors. That said, those factors alone will not be determinative in the typical DUI case. More important is the attorney's ability to dissect the facts, circumstances and evidence in the case itself.

Of course, if you have a low breath test that can be extrapolated to a lower result, or if there are issues with how the officer handled things on the scene, or you're facing some kind of enhancement for the breath test and we are attempting to get that reduced, what you've done with your personal life prior to the DUI can potentially make a difference.

What Is Your Process In Handling A DUI Case?

Generally, the first thing I do is talk with the client and get as much information as possible about what took place during the arrest. I look at the case on a step-by-step, minute-by-minute basis to understand every fact and circumstance in the events leading up to traffic stop, the DUI investigation, and the arrest itself. I also counsel clients on the procedures around the DHSMV and driver license consequences and assist the client in making the appropriate decisions related to that aspect of their DUI case.

When it comes to the criminal case I'll file a demand for discovery which means I'll seek all the evidence the State has in the case, like police reports, maintenance documents related to the breathalyzer machine, the citation, the arrest affidavit, and anything else that the State Attorney is relying on to bring a criminal charge of DUI. This importantly includes ordering a copy of the DUI video so that I can see what took place during the investigation. This not only allows me to view my client during the criminal investigation, but also the officer and check to see whether or not all appropriate and lawful process and procedure took place.

Once I have a chance to review the discovery I will evaluate all of the facts and circumstances to determine if there is a basis to file a motion to contest something the officers did or didn't do. For example, I could determine the traffic stop was bad or that the police didn't properly read and explain the implied consent rules surrounding the breath test, or that they didn't do a proper 20-minute observation before conducting a breath test and these would all be a basis for filing a motion. I have also seen cases where officers are seen coercing a client into performing Field Sobriety Tests which were then excluded from evidence against that client based on the fact that they were coerced. I will look through everything to see if there's a basis to file a motion and if so, I'll file it in an effort to get portions of the case thrown out.

If there doesn't seem to be a basis for a motion, but I think the client looks very good on the video, or if I think the way the client appears on video conflicts with the breath test results I'll put together a mitigation letter and present it to the State Attorney's Office.

The mitigation letter basically outlines what I believe the weaknesses are with the State Attorney's case along with painting a positive picture of my client. The goal here is to attempt to convince the State Attorney that they do not have a strong case and to convince them to reduce the charges to something other than a DUI. If the State Attorney won't agree to do that and we think we have a strong case, we'll set it for trial.

How Often Are You Able To Have DUI Charges Reduced Or Dismissed?

I am fortunate to have a lot of experience with DUI cases and I have a good reputation, so I think a fair amount of the time I am successful in getting charges reduced or dismissed, although it's really dependent on the jurisdiction and the facts and circumstances of the individual's case. For example, Pinellas County is very aggressive and tough on DUIs while Hillsborough County is somewhat more flexible. I always try my best to have my client's case reduced or dismissed, but again, the client's individual facts and circumstances are a significant factor in the outcome.

WHAT SETS YOUR FIRM APART IN HANDLING DUI CASES IN FLORIDA?

What sets us apart is the tremendous amount of experience that I bring to the table, both from a prosecution and a defense standpoint. I've handled every kind of DUI case from both sides of the table. Our firm spends a lot of listening to our clients and ensuring that we incorporate our client's voice into the case. We are very empathetic with our clients and we spend a tremendous amount of time breaking the case down and explaining every aspect of what our clients are facing to ensure they are a part of the process and are empowered during what is a very stressful situation. Personally, I have a very good professional reputation that I take a great deal of pride in, while at the same time I'm not afraid to push things as far as I need to in order to get the best result for a client. I believe that all of these factors set me, and our firm, apart from many other firms practicing DUI defense.

With our firm, you will get more attention and TLC, or concierge level service, than you'll get with the Public Defender's office or other private defense firms in town. With our firm, you can call us any time to get questions answered, or you can come in the office for a face-to-face meeting with your attorney or you can e-mail or text us.

Those things are just simply not available with the Public Defender's office and don't necessarily happen consistently with other private defense firms. Typically, a client will only see a Public Defender when they actually go to court - outside of that, it's extremely difficult to reach them to speak about your case proactively. We hear from many clients that come from other private defense firms that their attorneys were inattentive and/or difficult to reach, or simply didn't spend enough time explaining their case to them. We do our very best to ensure every client is treated like our only client.

We are often asked why not save attorney fees and simply use the Public Defender from a cost perspective. Although there are good attorneys in the Public Defender's office, you are assigned a Public Defender – you are not in control and are not making the choice yourself. When you hire our firm, you're making a choice based on the experience and background of the attorney, and also making sure that their personality fits with yours, which is important, since you'll be working with the attorney for quite some time. DUI cases can drag on for months regardless of the attorney's efforts to resolve it quickly. It is important that you have a personality fit with your attorney and the firm at large, and that you are hiring someone that you feel you can trust and be assured that they will do their best for you on your case.

Are There Any Case Studies That You Would Like To Share?

I once represented a woman who was older (in her 60s) and she had absolutely no prior record and she just was a fabulous woman who had served in the military for most of her life, and she had a very good upbringing and background. Unfortunately, she ended up in a traffic accident with a motorcyclist who lost the use of his legs. She had left the scene of the accident to go back to a restaurant to get help. Once at the restaurant she told the people at the restaurant what happened and they called the police. Even though she had sought help and had not tried to hide or minimize her involvement in the accident she was still ultimately charged with DUI Serious Bodily Injury, and Leaving the Scene of an Accident With Injury. Again, she had never been in trouble before but the State still aggressively prosecuted her case and sought a five-year prison sentence on her. This terrified her and she would call me once a week crying and I spent a lot of time trying to talk her through it.

Ultimately, I was able to successfully litigate the case in front of the judge and she was given probation with no prison. The judge departed from the law, which called for prison, and agreed to depart from the statutory guidelines and not impose any type of incarceration – over the State's objection. The client completed her probation and spent no time in jail which was a very successful outcome for the client.

This is why it's important to have an attorney represent your case, because attorneys not only represent the facts and circumstances of the case and argue matters of law for you, they also represent you as an individual, and the example of this case has a lot to do with that. It's about learning as much about your client as possible; learning about their background and who they are as a person, and representing that appropriately to the State's Attorney's office and the court to make the case not just about the facts, circumstances and the law, which is unbelievably important, but also making the case about who the client is, so the court sees the individual involved in the event, including the positive aspects of that individual, their life and their family background, which can weigh into the decisions of the State and the court. That's an important reason to have an advocate on your side to do just that.

DISCLAIMER

This publication is intended to be informational only. No legal advice is being given, and no attorney-client relationship is intended to be created by reading this material. If you are facing legal issues, whether criminal or civil, seek professional legal counsel to get your questions answered.

Morris Law Firm, P.A.

111 2nd Avenue NE, Suite #515

St. Petersburg, Florida 33701

(727) 388-4736

www.criminalattorneystpetersburg.com

Made in the USA
Monee, IL
05 November 2026

67385051R00050